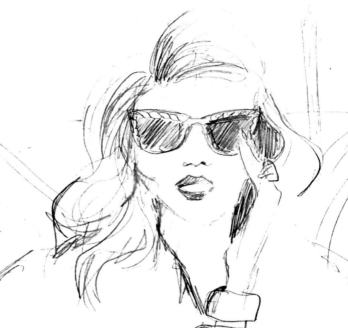

Printed in the United States of America

First Printing, 2016

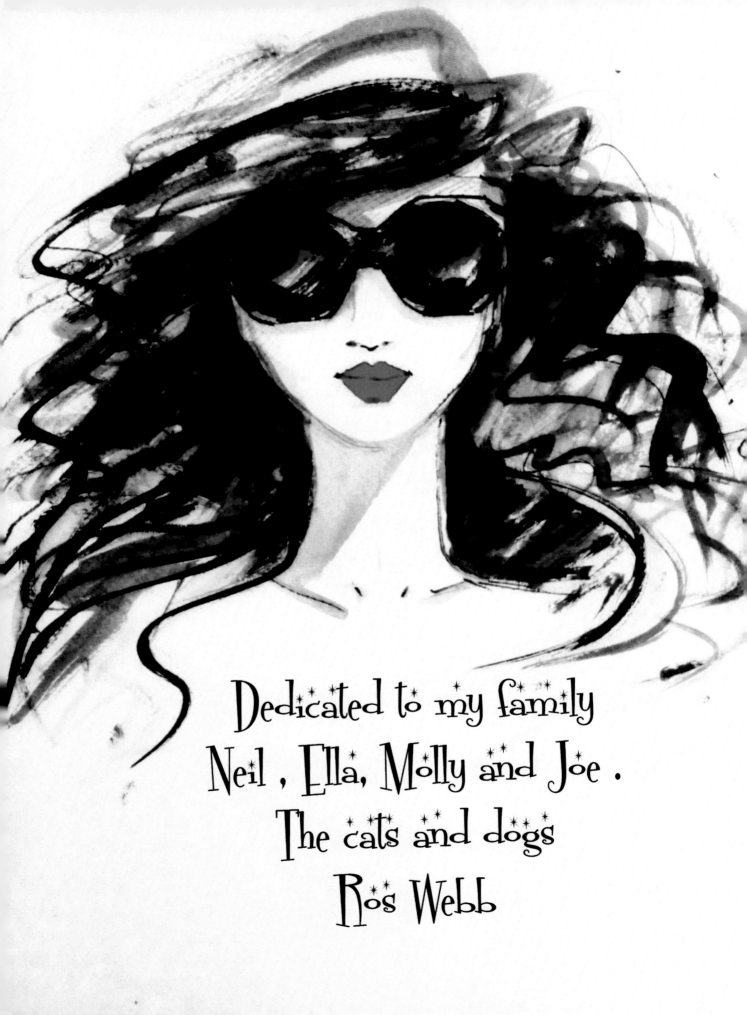

Dedicated to my family
Neil , Ella, Molly and Joe .
The cats and dogs
Ros Webb

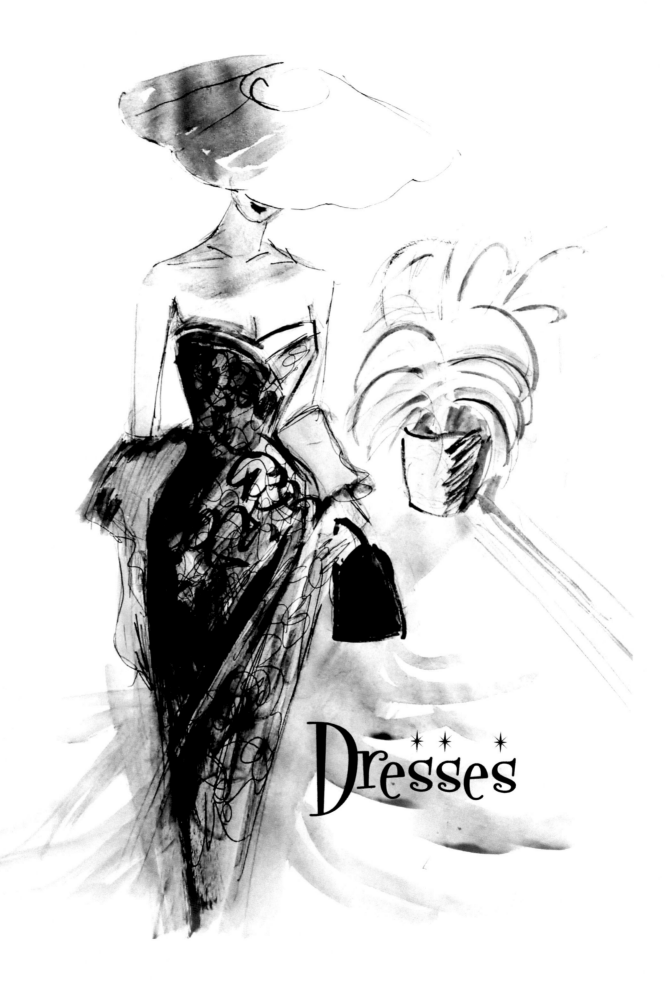

Dresses

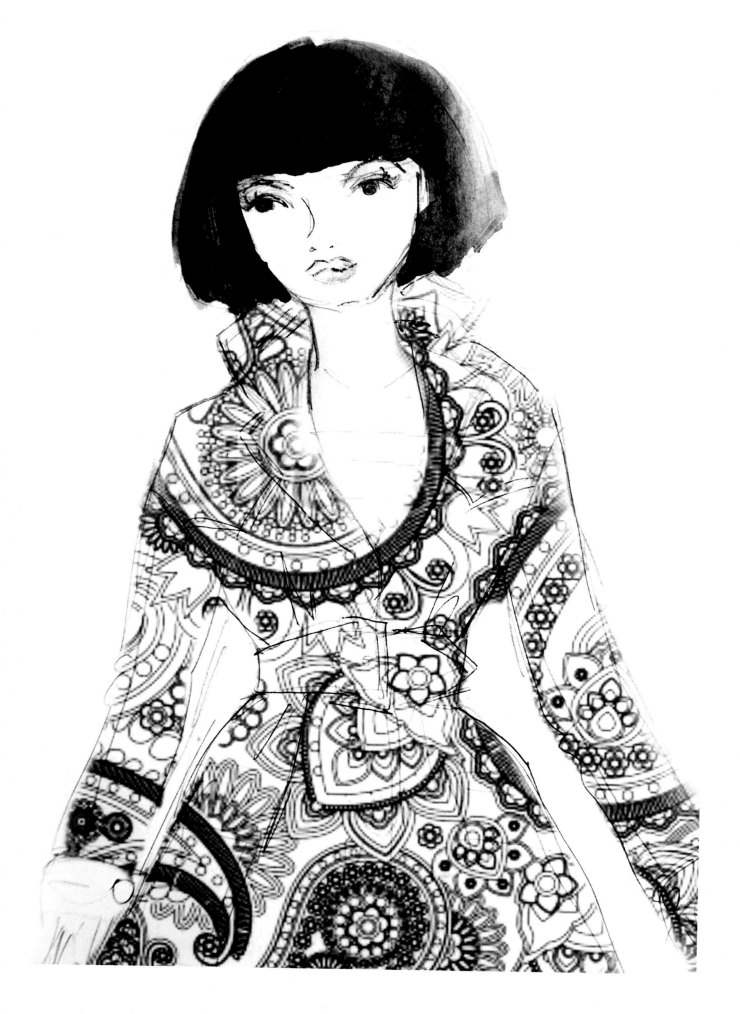

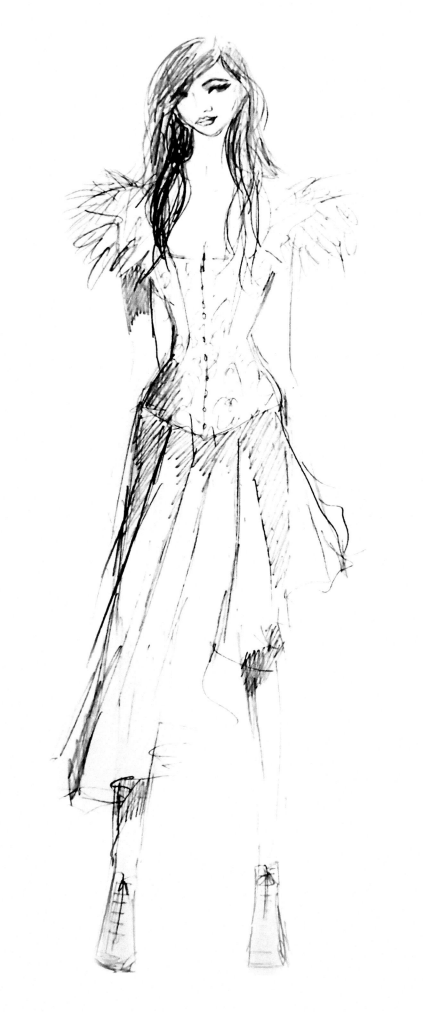

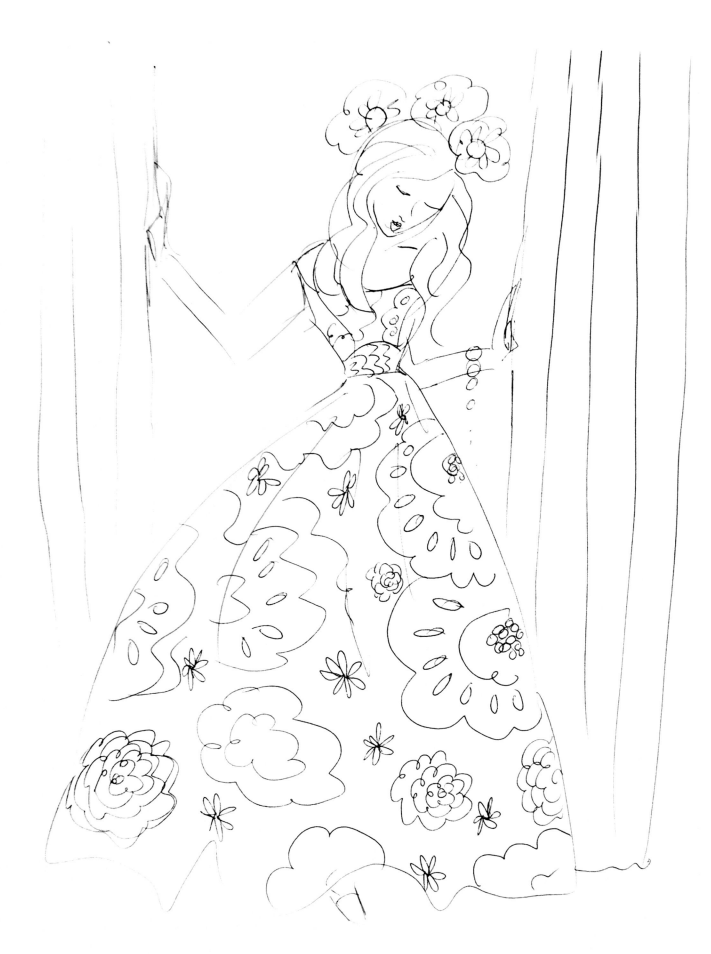

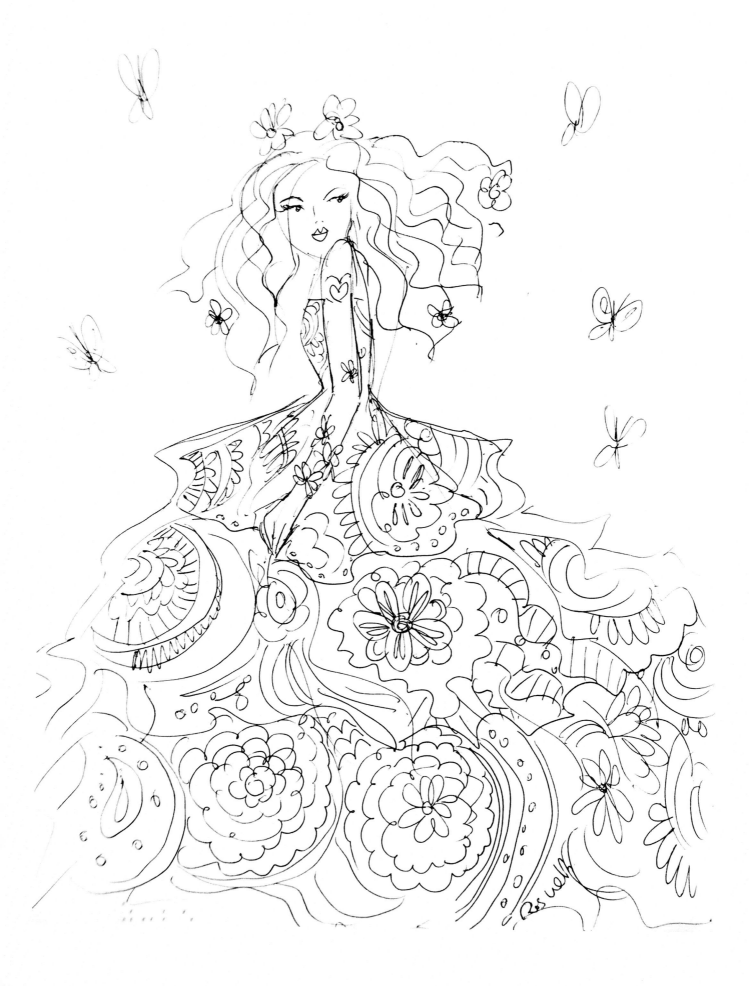

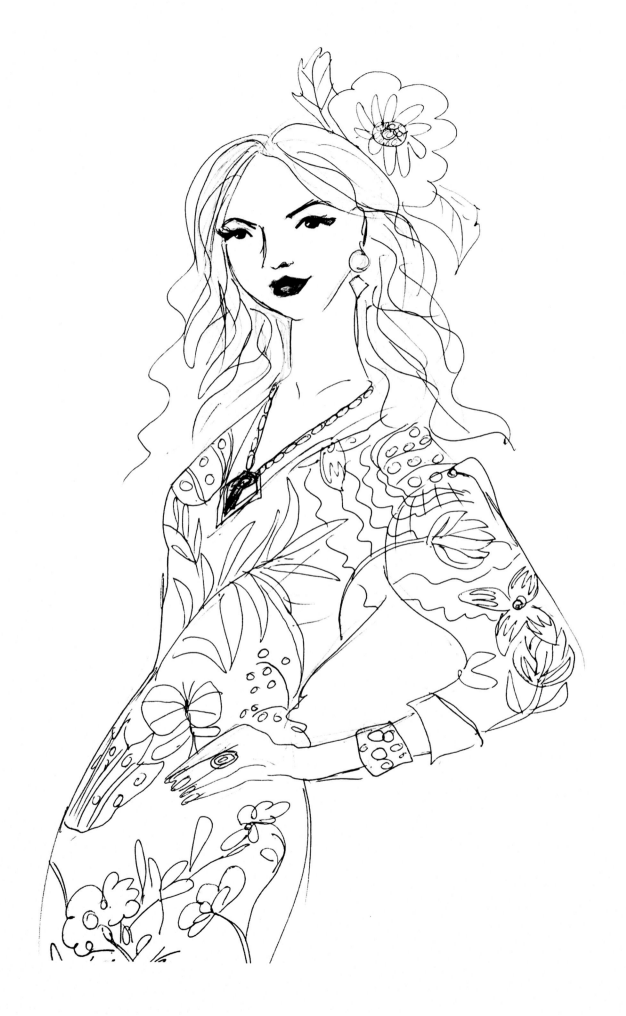

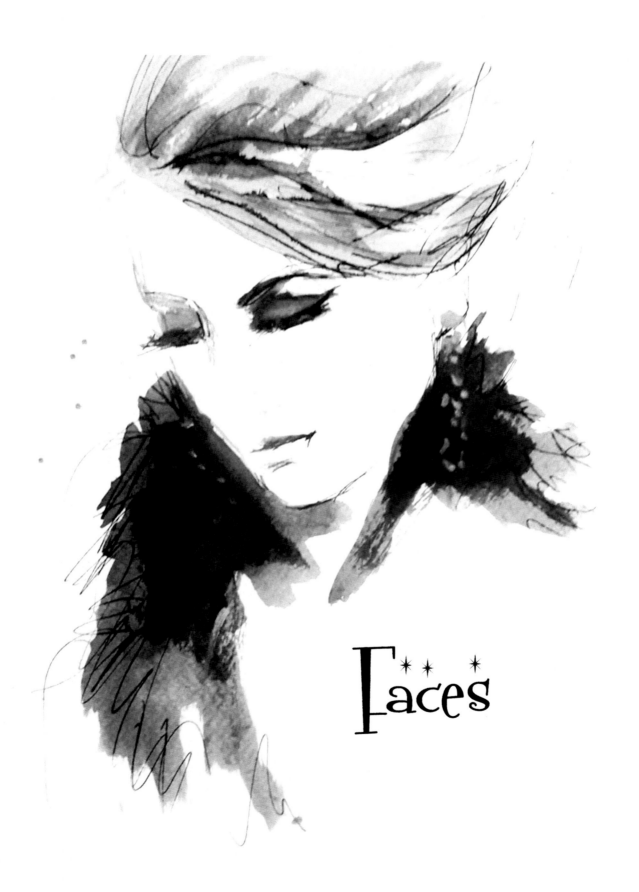

Faces

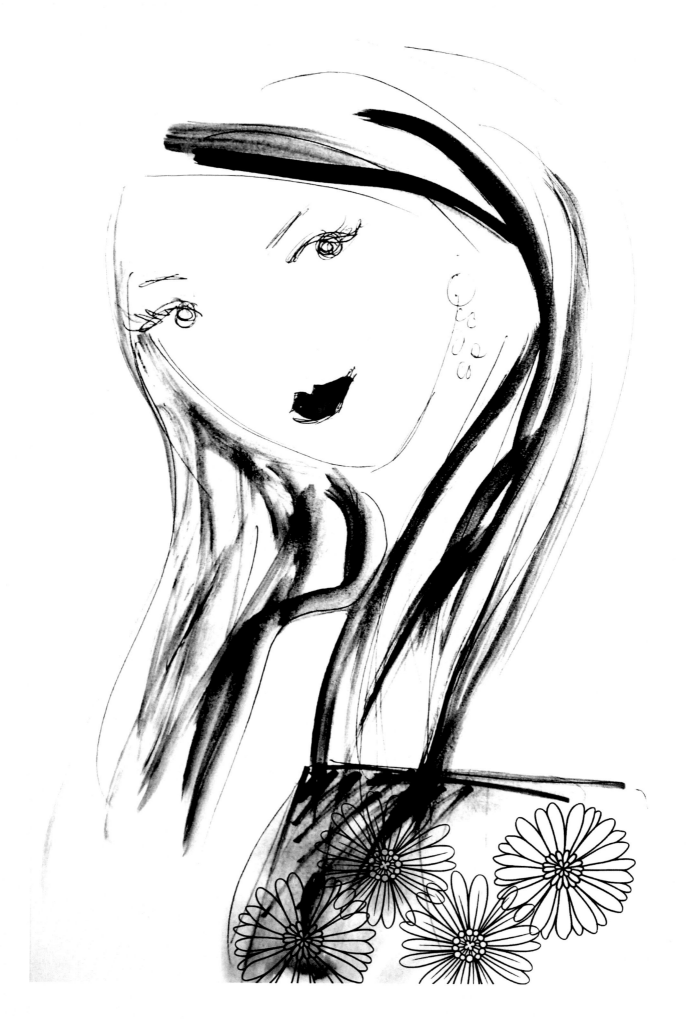

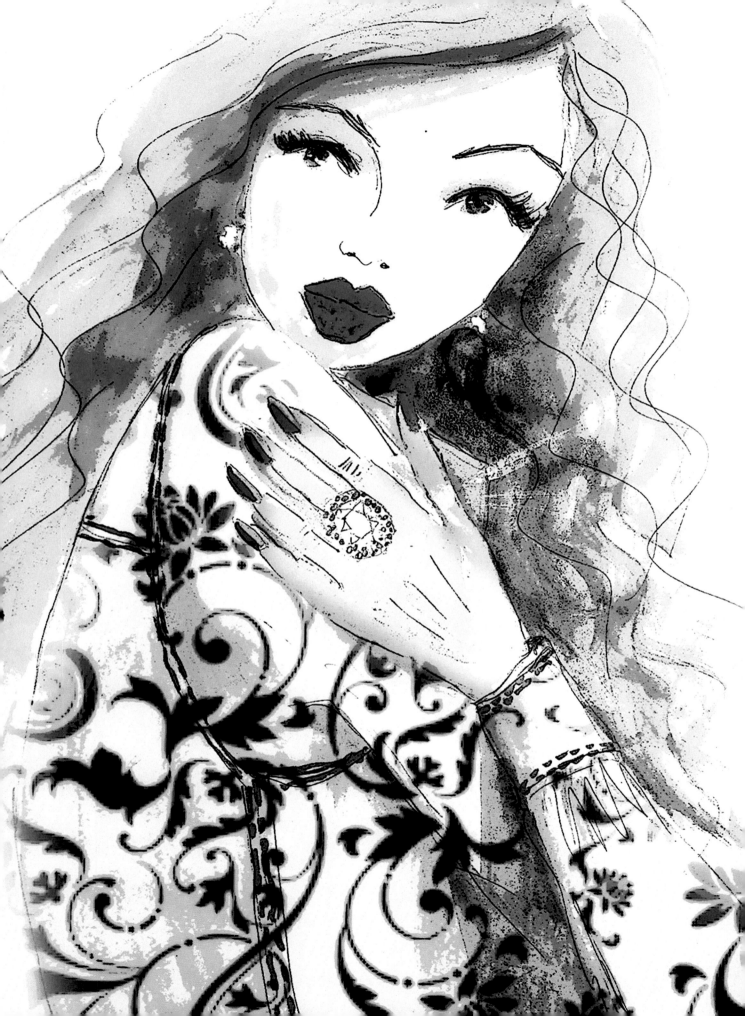

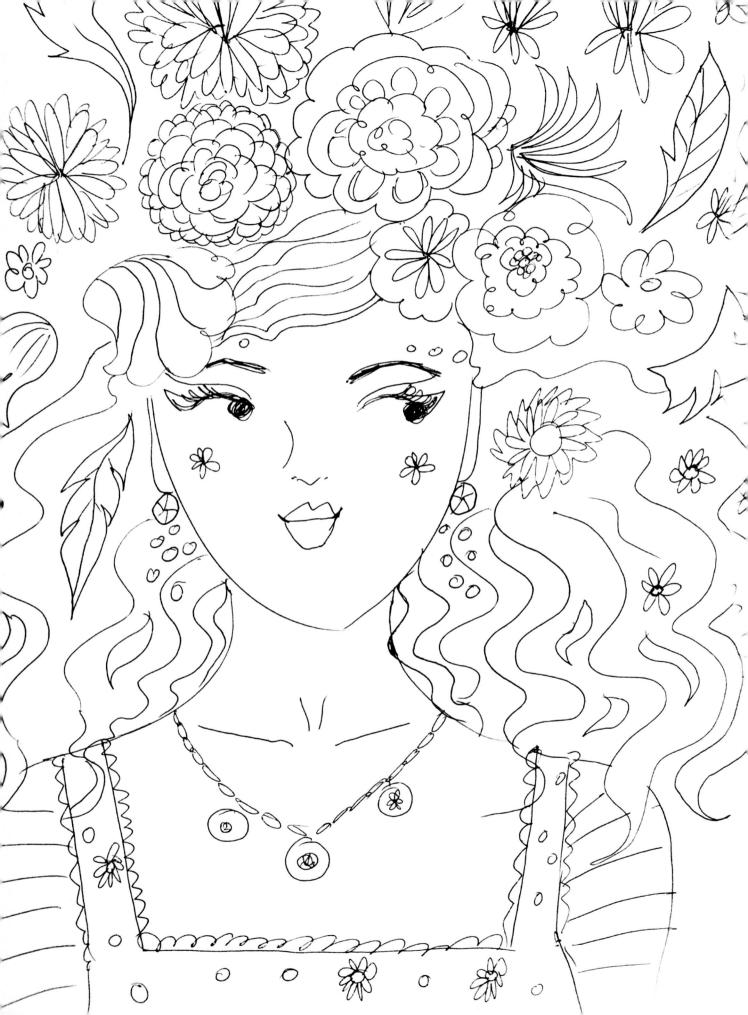

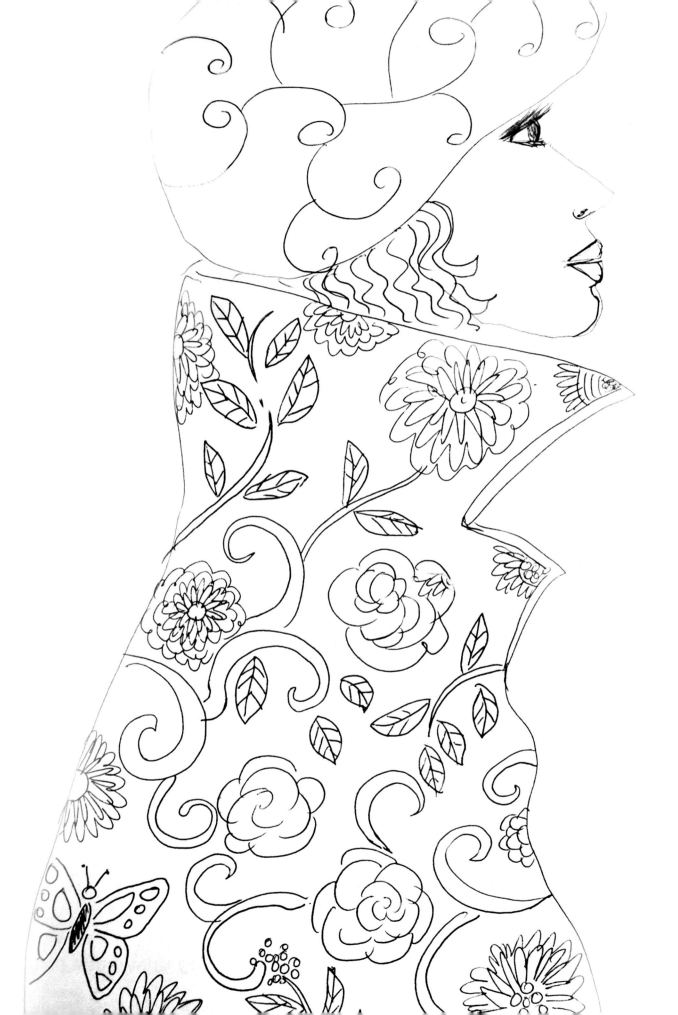

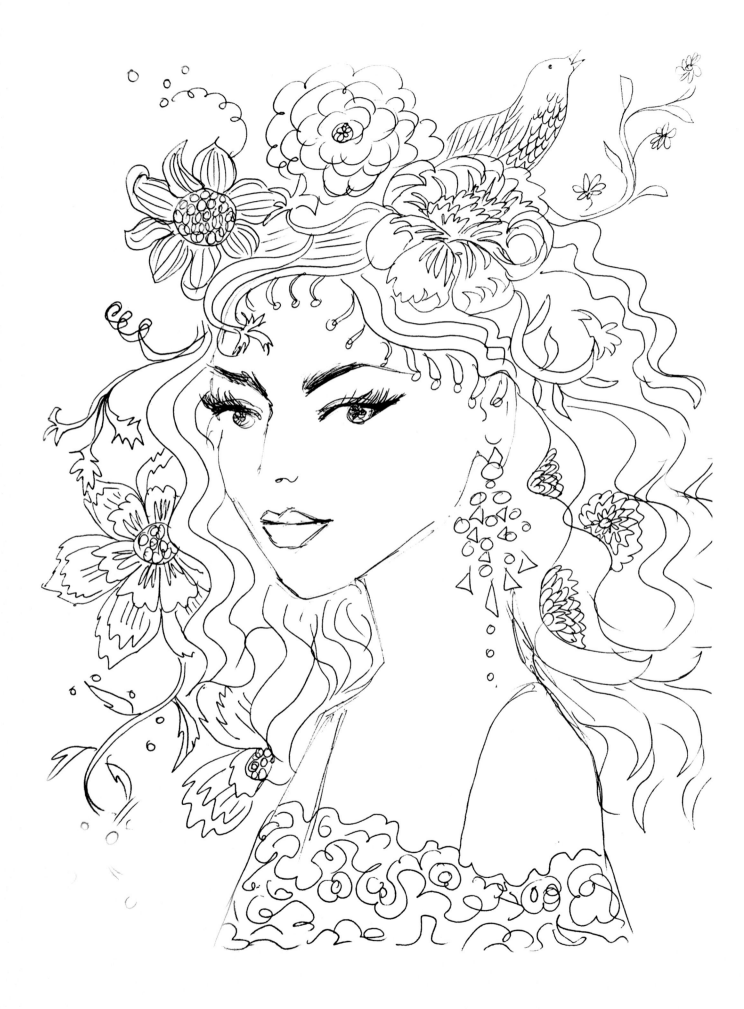

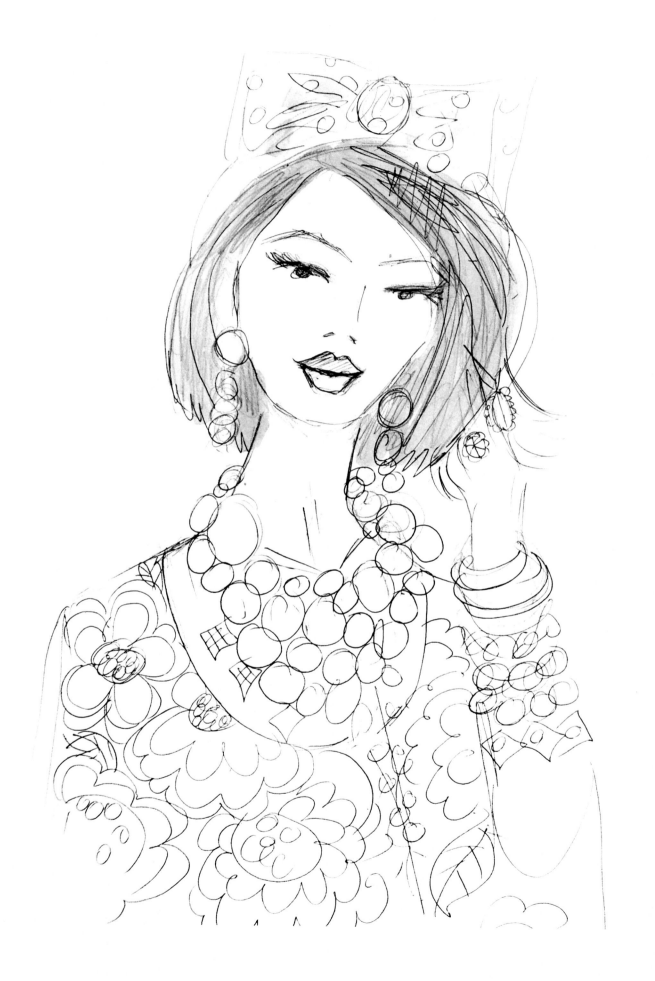

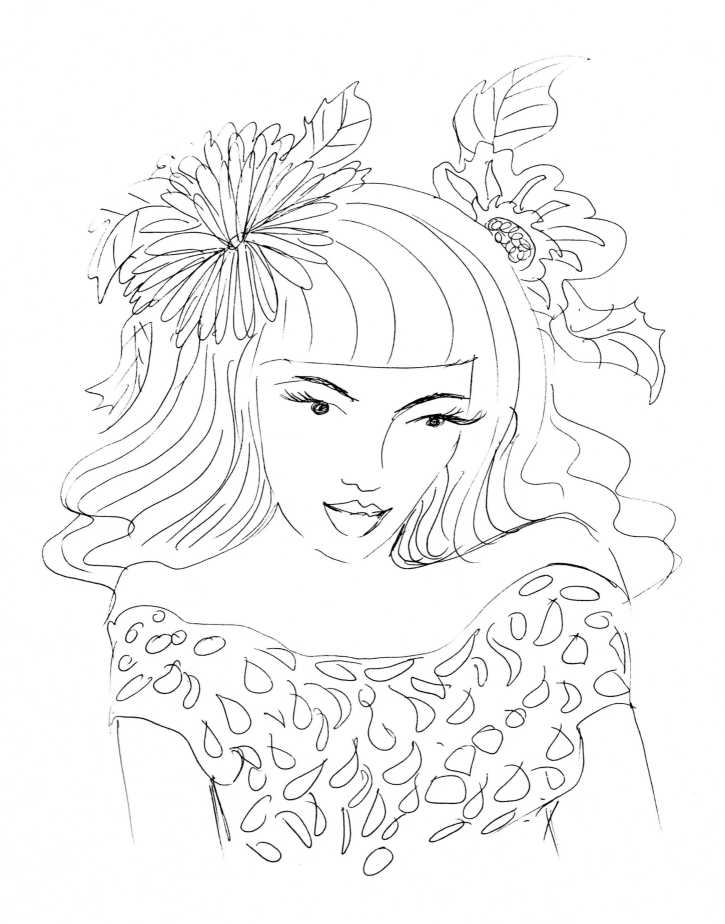

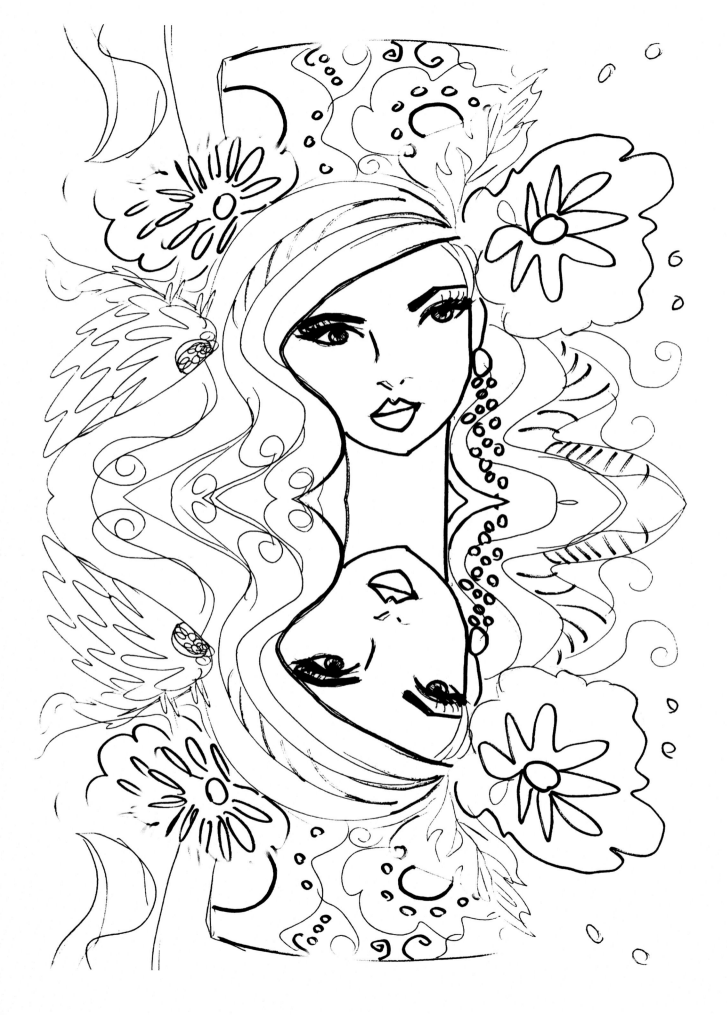

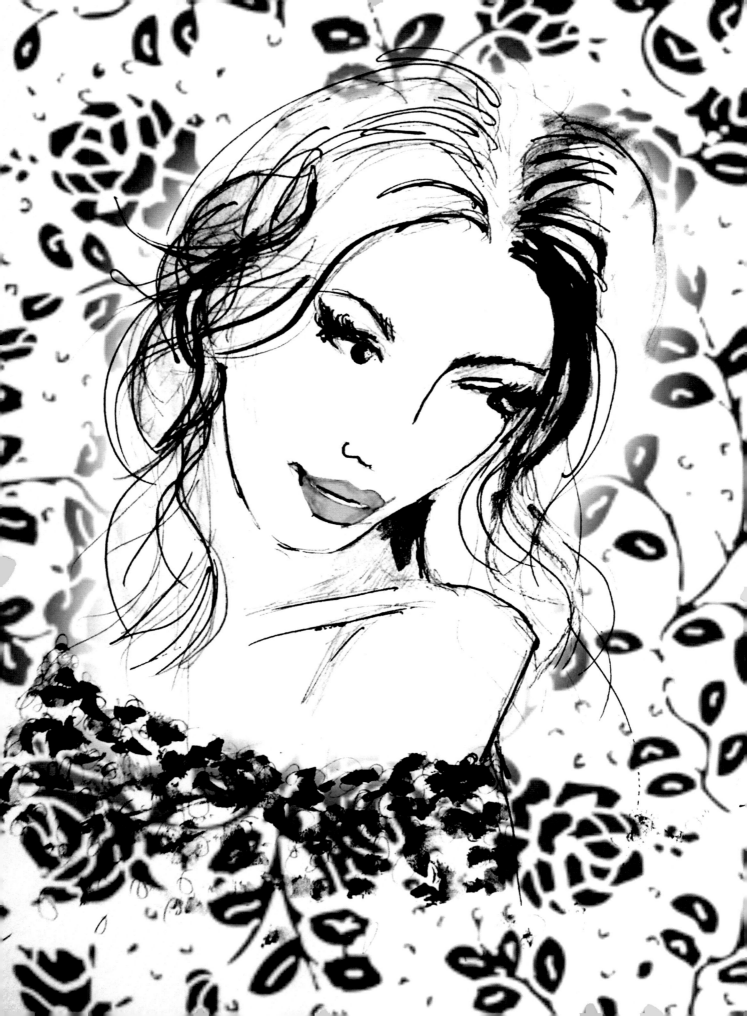

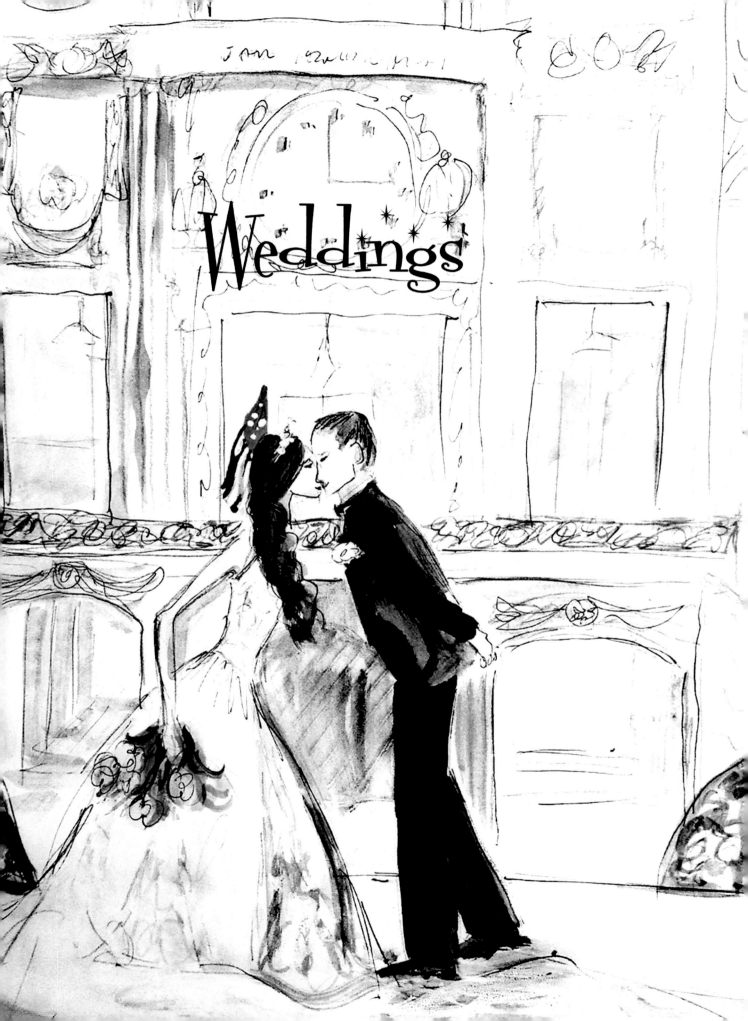

Weddings

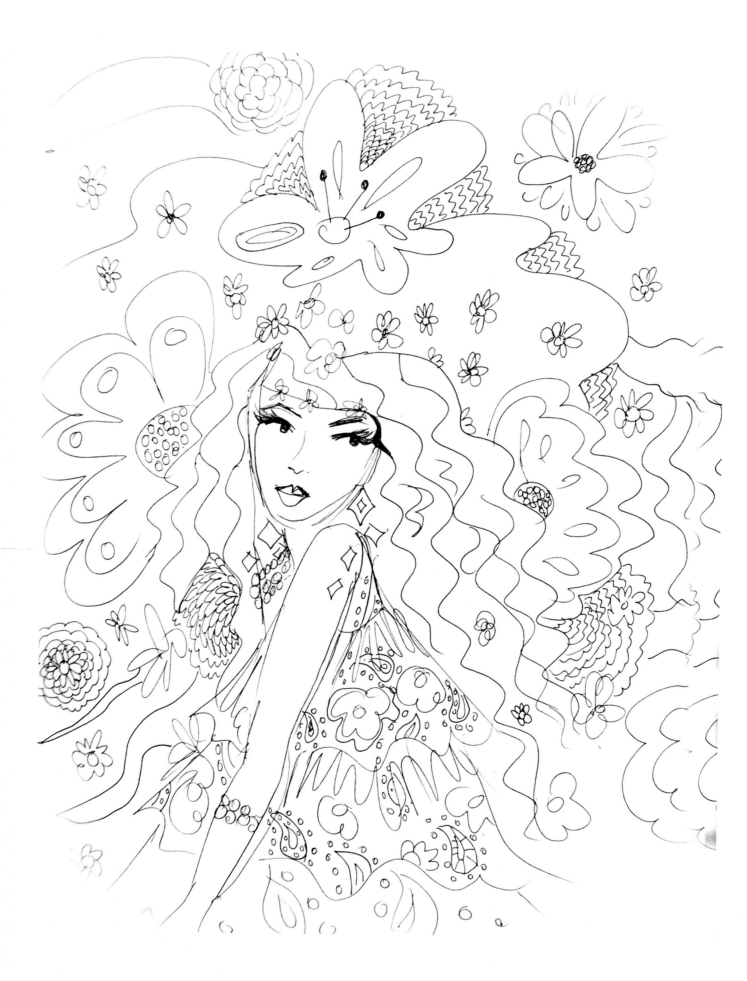

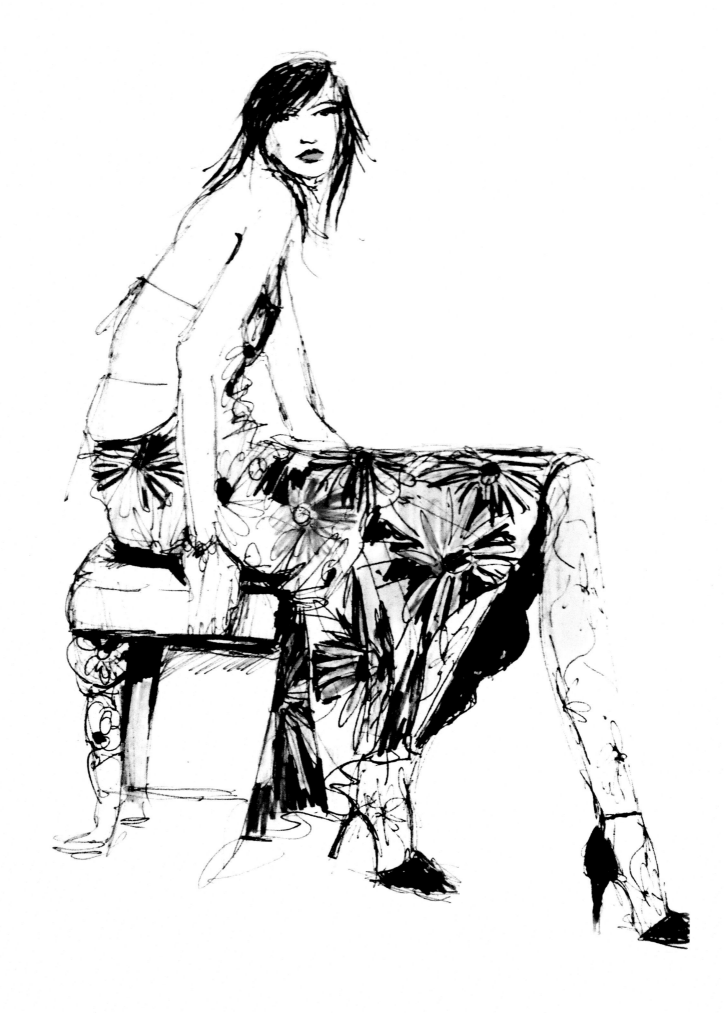

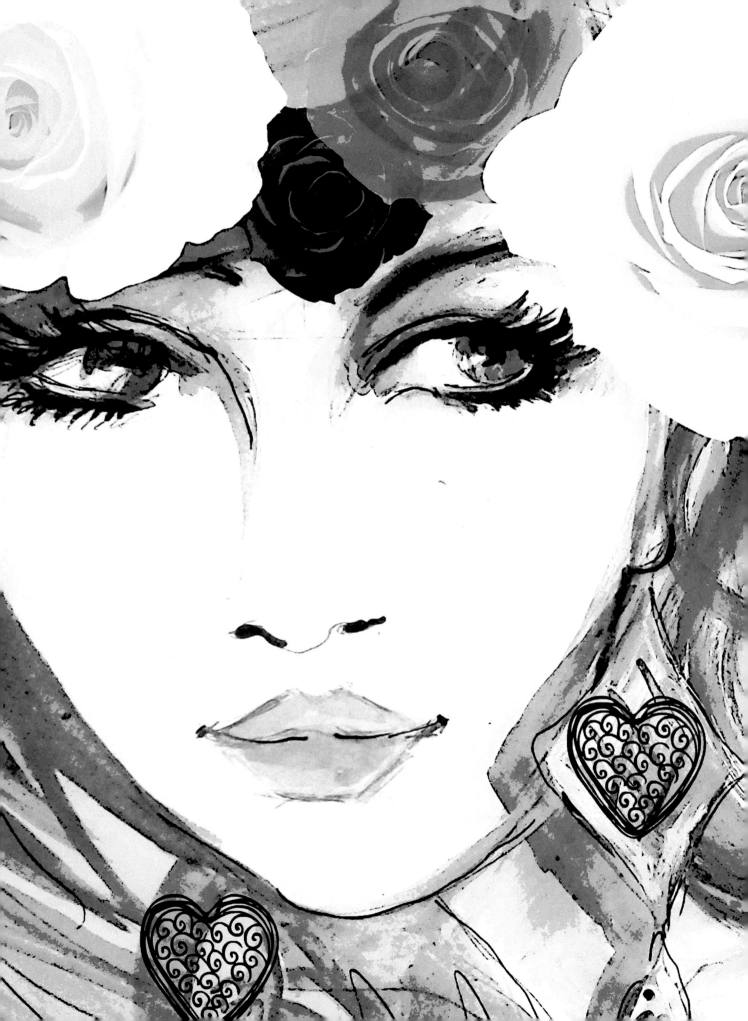

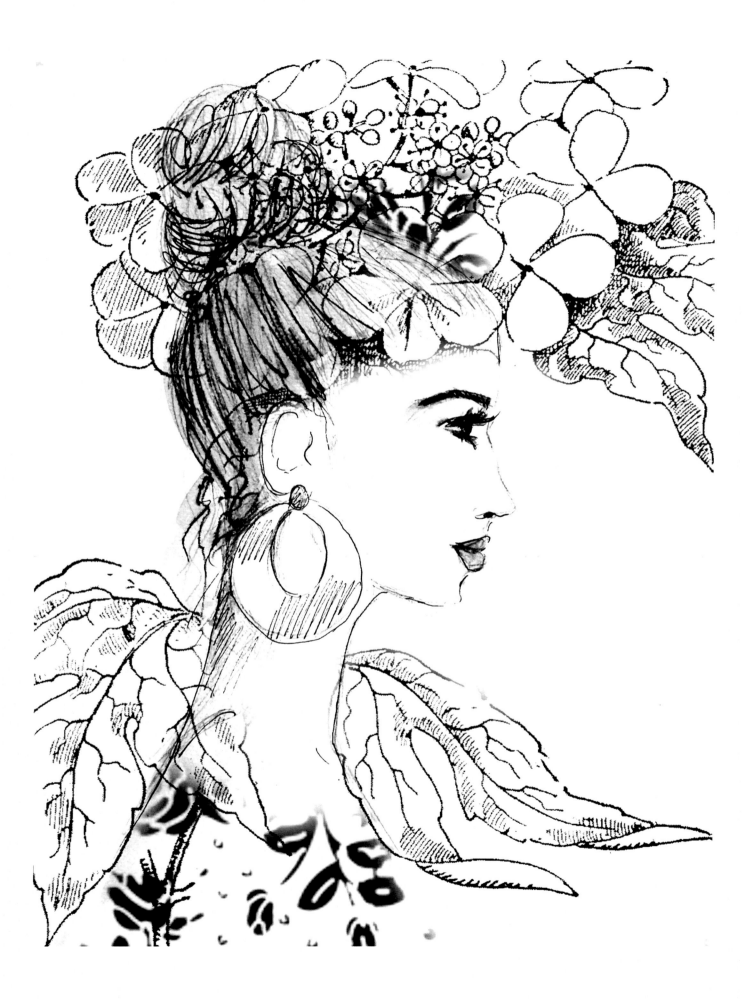

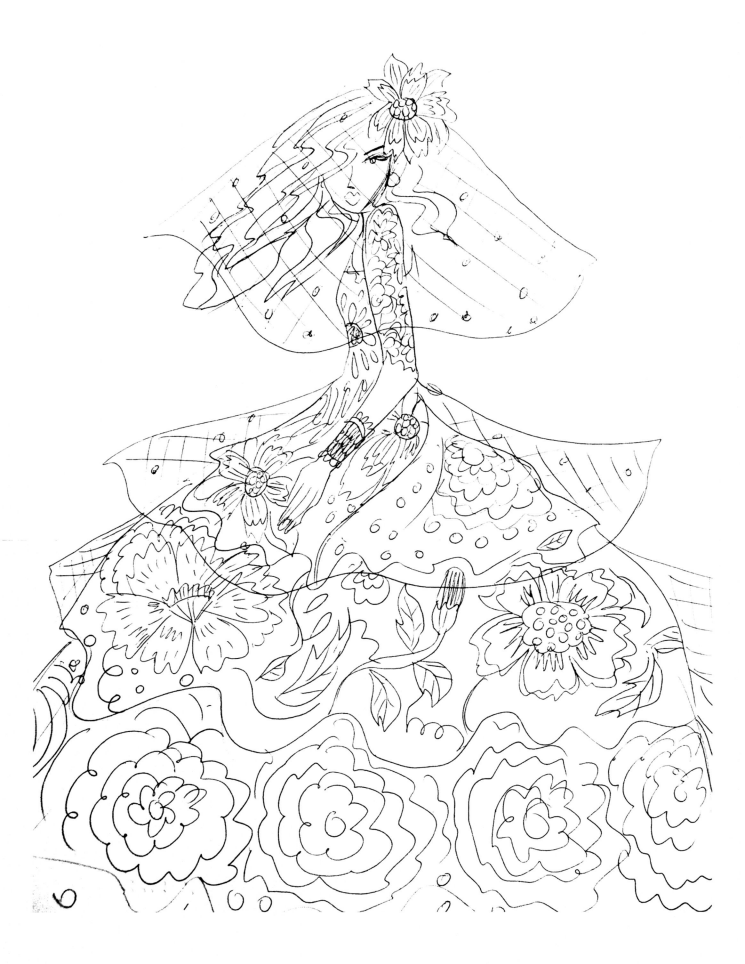

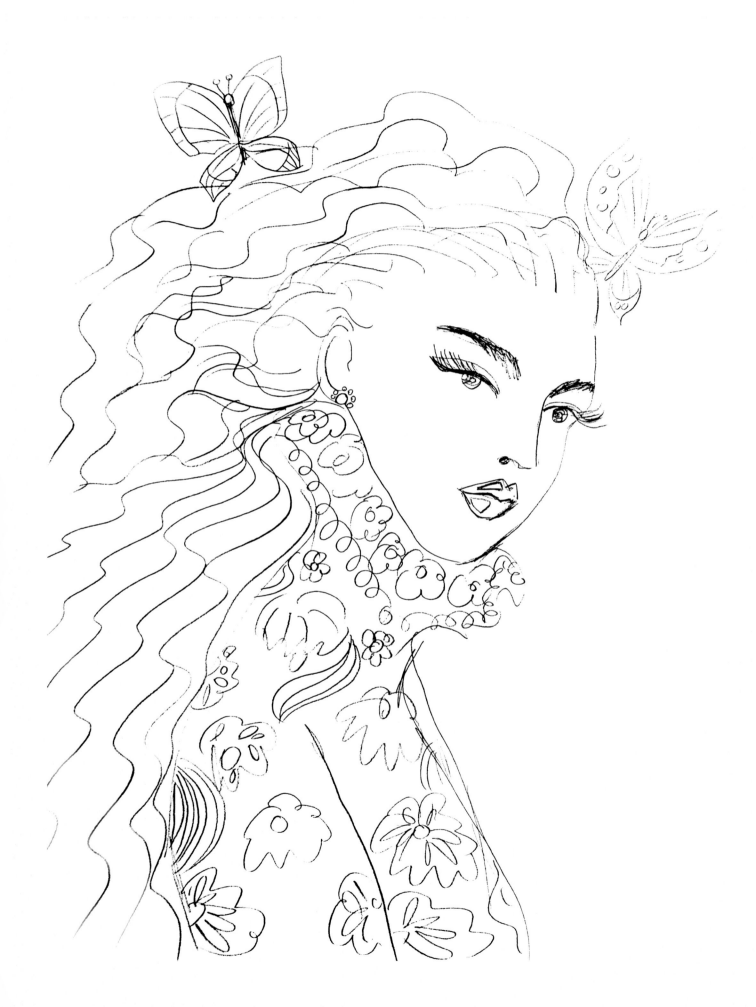

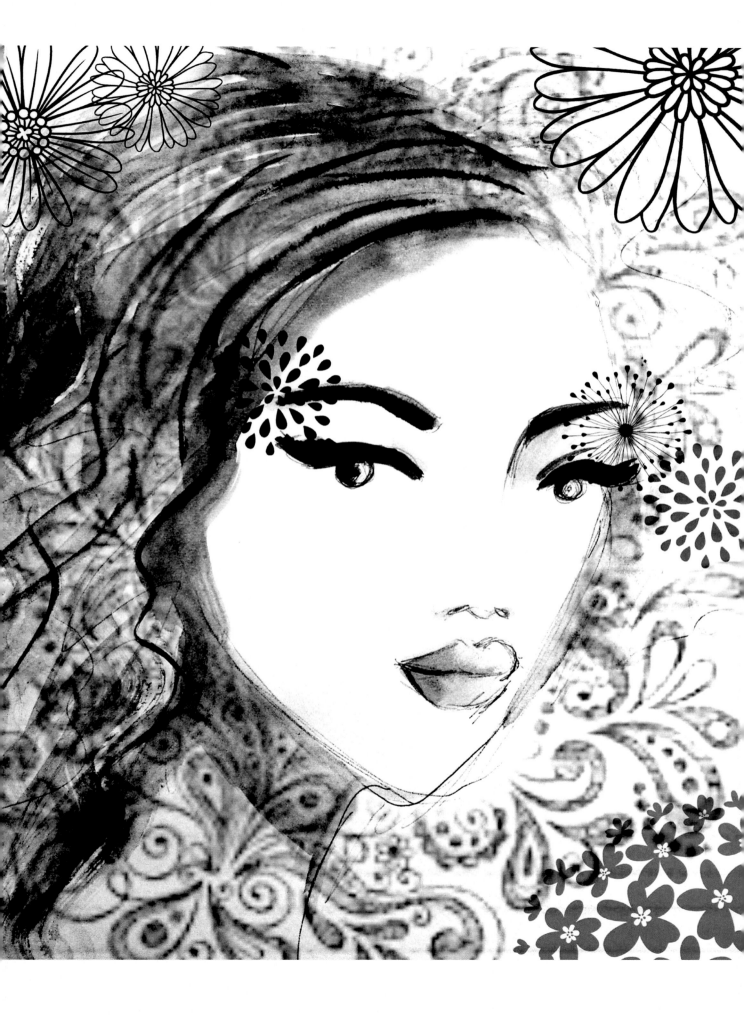

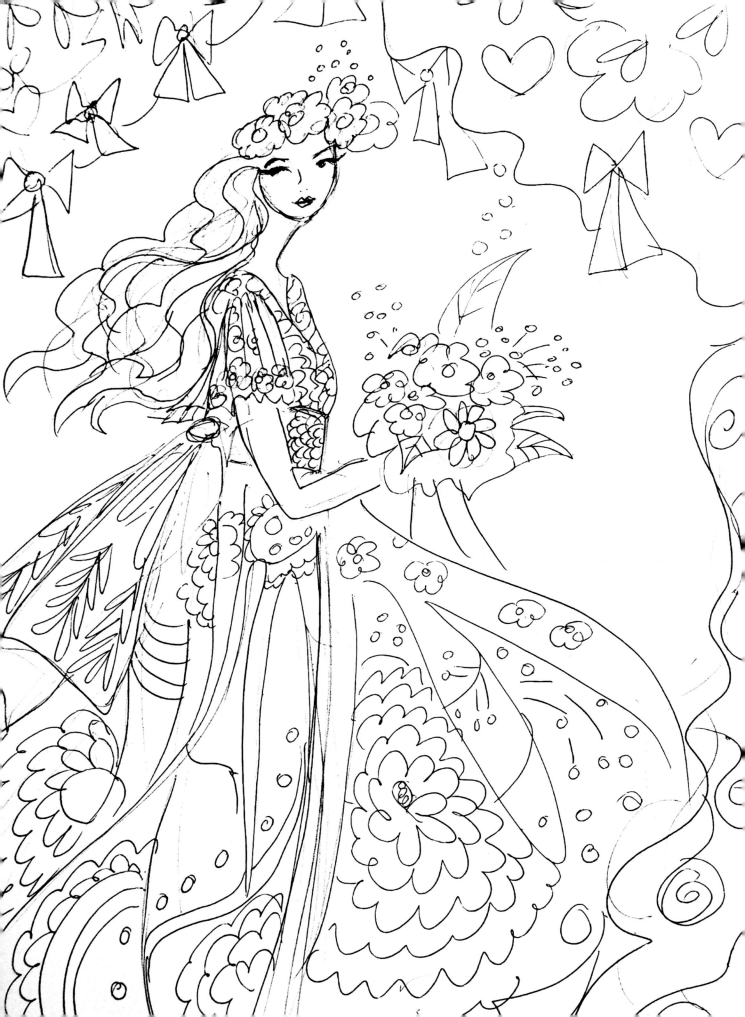

# City Life

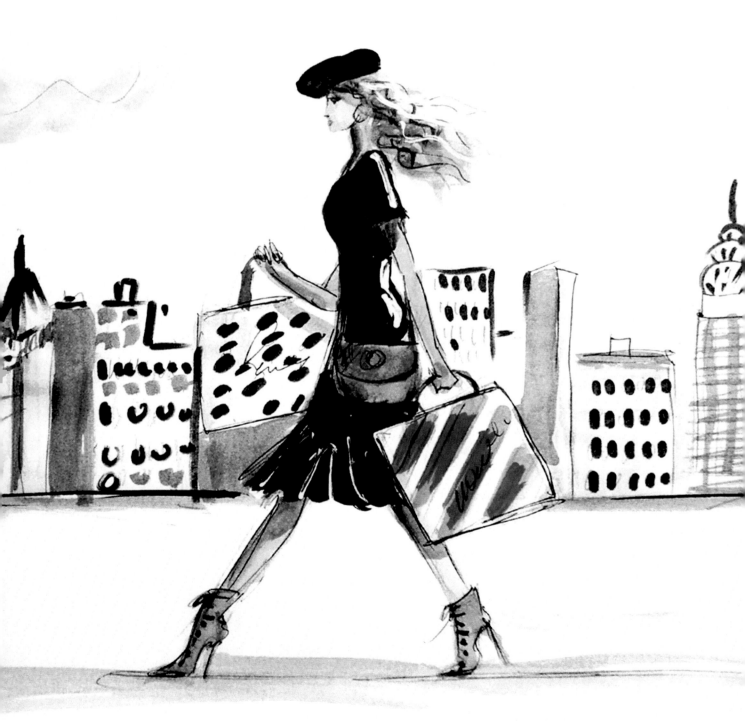

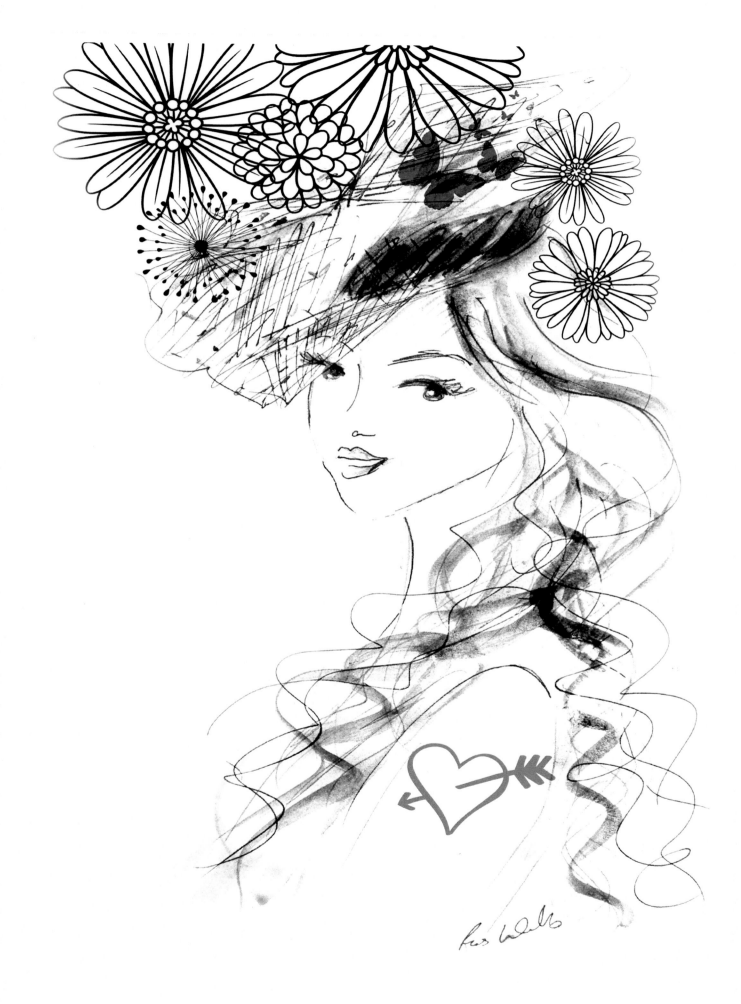

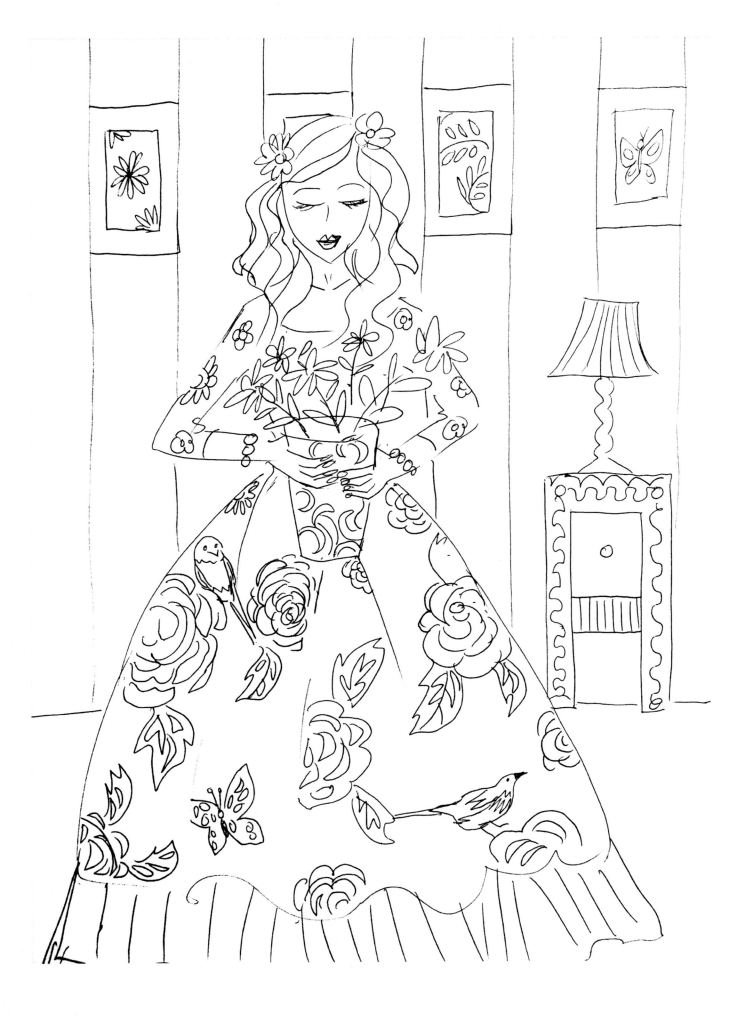

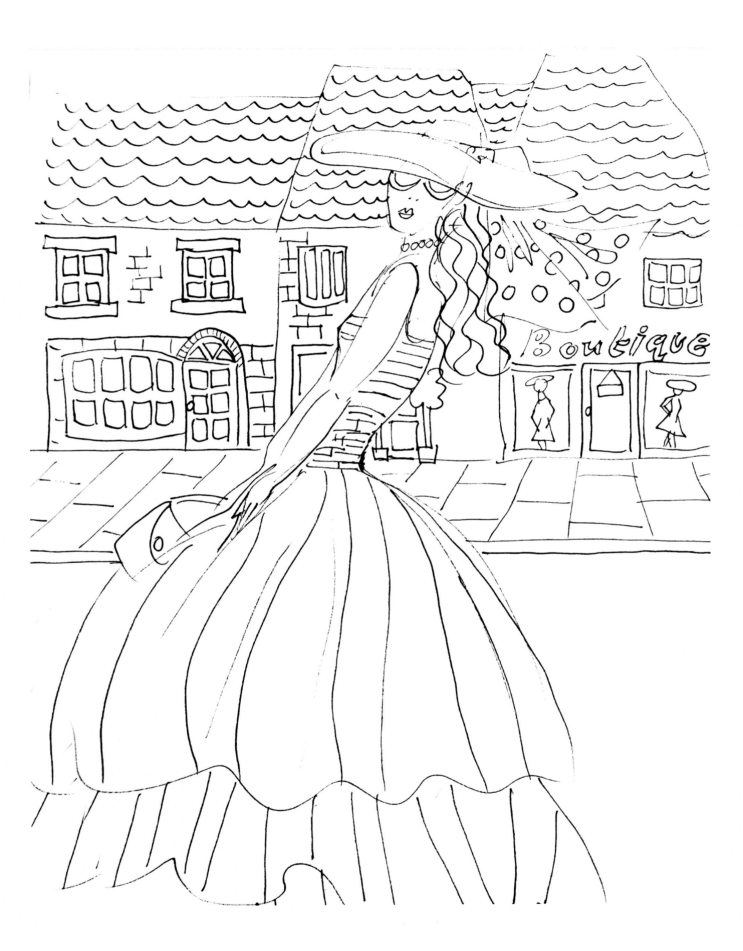

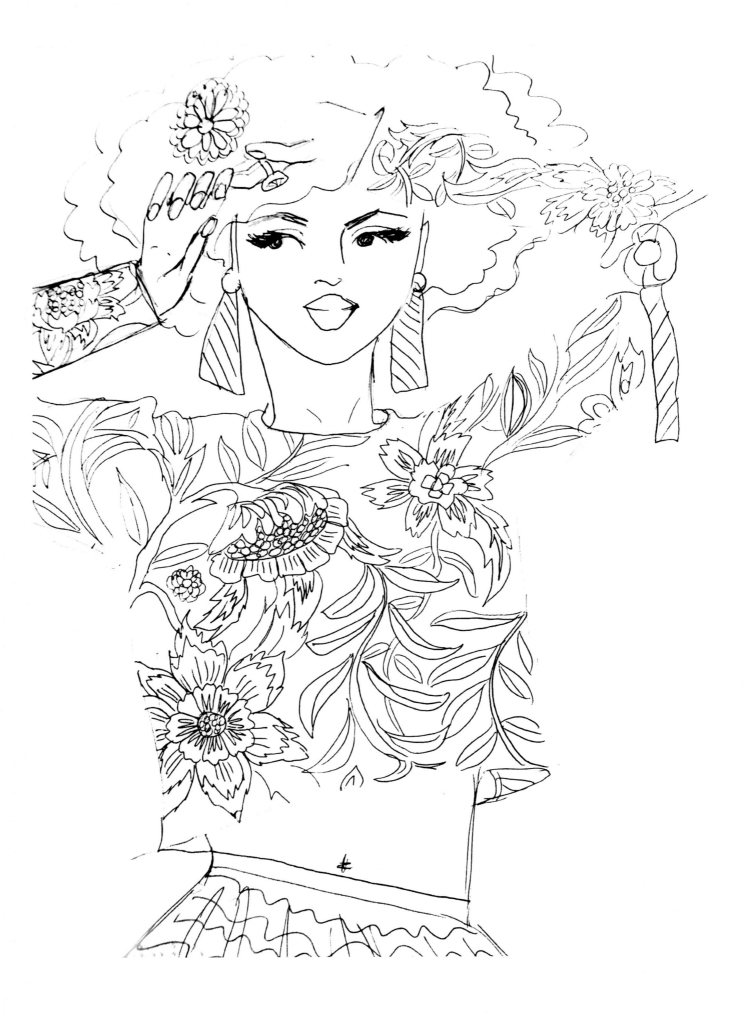

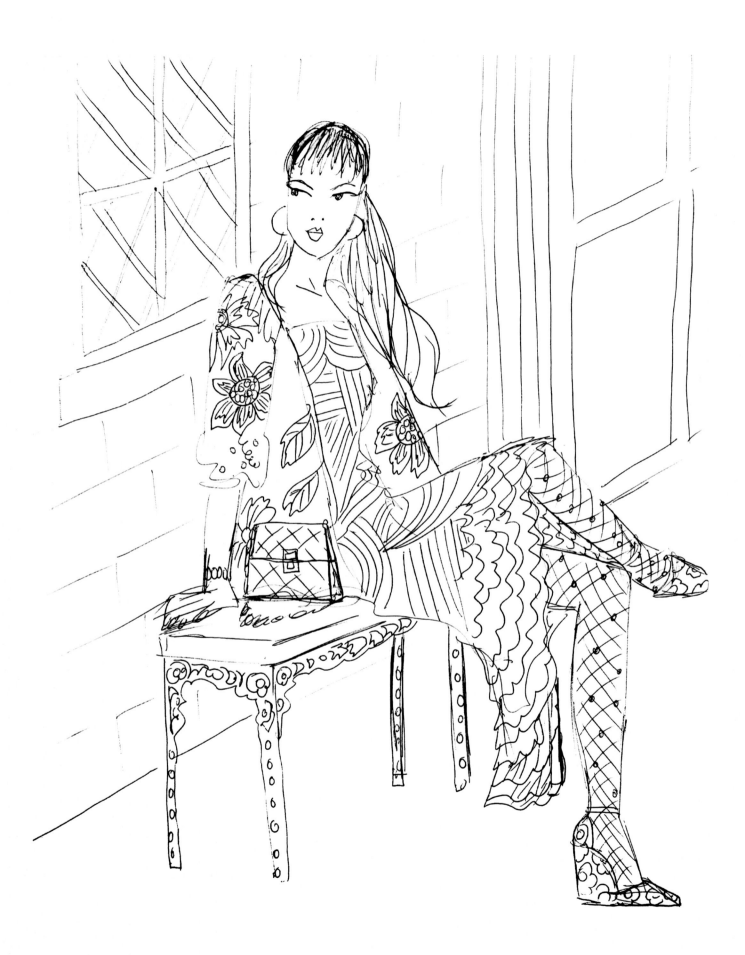

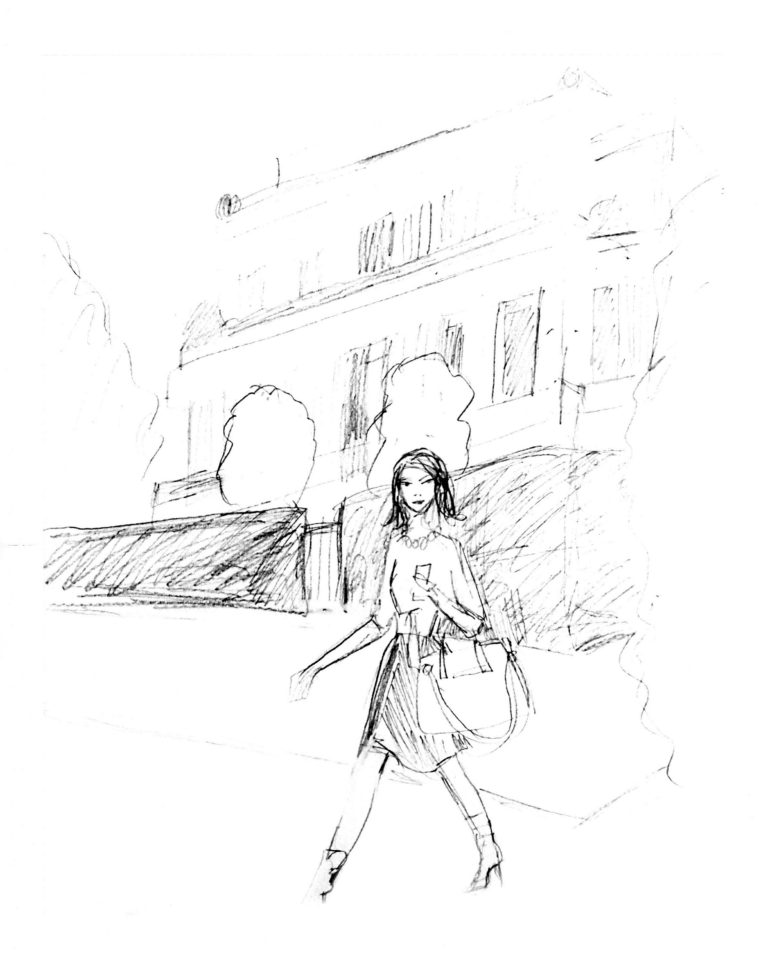

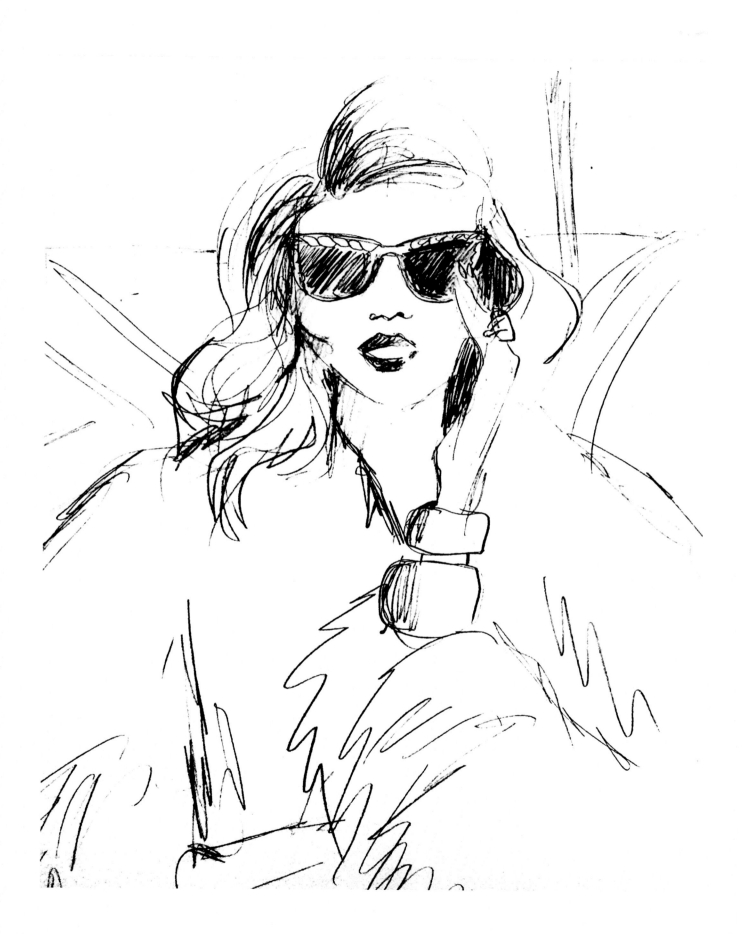

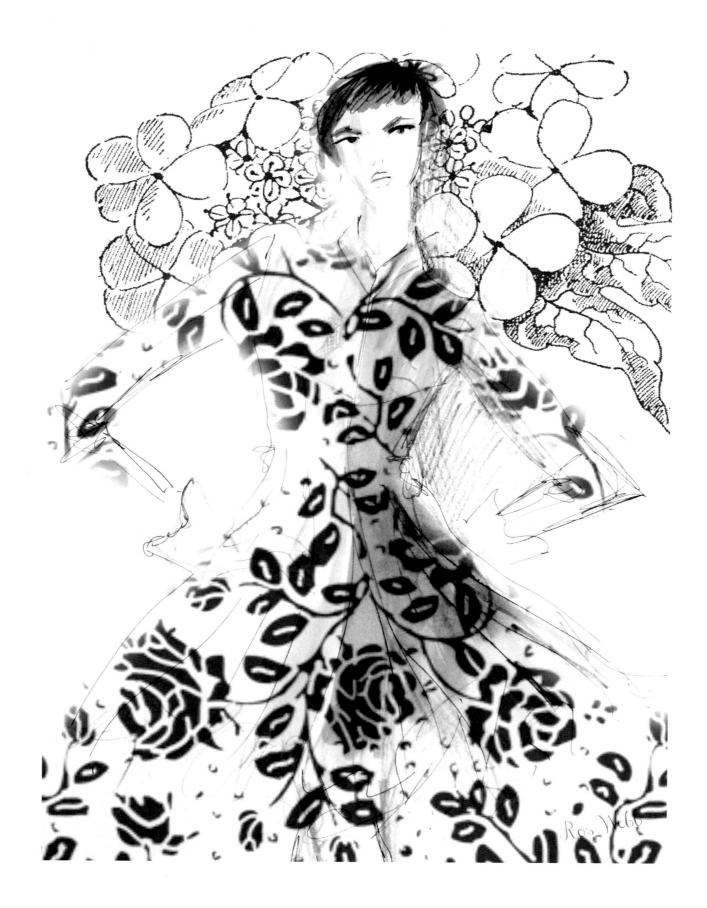

Made in United States
Orlando, FL
21 December 2024

56368500R00040